#2016-082

UNITED STATES OF AMERICA
DEPARTMENT OF THE TREASURY
COMPTROLLER OF THE CURRENCY

	)
In the Matter of:	)
	)
Wells Fargo Bank, N.A.	)
Sioux Falls, South Dakota	)
	)

AA-EC-2016-69

CONSENT ORDER FOR A CIVIL MONEY PENALTY

The Office of the Comptroller of the Currency ("Comptroller" or "OCC"), through his national bank examiners, has examined the affairs of Wells Fargo Bank, N.A., Sioux Falls, South Dakota ("Bank"), and has identified: (1) violations of the Servicemembers Civil Relief Act ("SCRA"), 50 U.S.C. §§ 3901-4043, and (2) deficiencies in the Bank's program for compliance with the SCRA. The Comptroller has informed the Bank of the findings resulting from its examinations.

The Bank, by and through its duly elected and acting Board of Directors ("Board"), has executed a Stipulation and Consent to the Issuance of an Order for a Civil Money Penalty, dated September 29, 2016, that is accepted by the Comptroller ("Stipulation"). By this Stipulation, which is incorporated herein by reference, the Bank has consented to the issuance of this Consent Order for a Civil Money Penalty ("Order") by the Comptroller.

ARTICLE I

COMPTROLLER'S FINDINGS

The Comptroller finds, and the Bank neither admits nor denies, the following:

(1) Between approximately 2007 and 2014, the Bank failed to apply the six percent interest rate cap to certain servicemember[1] obligations and liabilities, in violation of 50 U.S.C. § 3937(a)(1);

(2) Between approximately 2006 and 2011, the Bank failed to accurately disclose servicemembers' military status in certain affidavits filed in those servicemembers' eviction proceedings, in violation of 50 U.S.C. § 3931(b)(1).

(3) Between approximately 2007 and 2016, the Bank failed to obtain court orders prior to repossessing certain servicemembers' automobiles, in violation of 50 U.S.C. § 3952(a)(1).

(4) The Bank's conduct, as described in Paragraphs (1) through (3) of this Article, were part of a pattern of misconduct.

(5) The Bank's conduct, as described in Paragraphs (1) through (3) of this Article, resulted in financial gain to the Bank.

Pursuant to the authority vested in him by the Federal Deposit Insurance Act, as amended, 12 U.S.C. § 1818(i), the Comptroller hereby ORDERS that:

ARTICLE II

ORDER FOR A CIVIL MONEY PENALTY

(1) The Bank shall make payment of a civil money penalty in the total amount of 20 million dollars ($20,000,000), which shall be paid upon the execution of this Order:

 (a) If a check is the selected method of payment, the check shall be made payable to the Treasurer of the United States and shall be delivered to:

---

[1] As used in this Order, the term "servicemember" is the same as defined by the SCRA, 50 U.S.C. § 3911(1).

Comptroller of the Currency, P.O. Box 979012, St. Louis, Missouri 63197-9000.

(b) If a wire transfer is the selected method of payment, it shall be sent in accordance with instructions provided by the Comptroller.

(c) The docket number of this case (AA-EC-2016-69) shall be entered on the payment document or wire confirmation and a photocopy of the payment document or confirmation of the wire transfer shall be sent immediately, by overnight delivery, to the Director of Enforcement and Compliance, Office of the Comptroller of the Currency, 400 7th Street, S.W., Washington, D.C. 20219.

(2) This Order shall be enforceable to the same extent and in the same manner as an effective and outstanding order that has been issued and has become final pursuant to 12 U.S.C. § 1818.

ARTICLE III

OTHER PROVISIONS

(1) This Order is intended to be, and shall be construed to be, a final order issued pursuant to 12 U.S.C. § 1818(i)(2), and expressly does not form, and may not be construed to form, a contract binding on the OCC or the United States.

(2) This Order constitutes a settlement of the civil money penalty proceeding against the Bank contemplated by the Comptroller, based on the violations of the SCRA described in the Comptroller's Findings set forth in Article I of this Order. The Comptroller releases and discharges the Bank from all potential liability for a civil money penalty that has been or might have been asserted by the Comptroller based on the violations of the SCRA described in the

Comptroller's Findings set forth in Article I of this Order, to the extent known to the Comptroller as of the effective date of this Order. Nothing in the Stipulation or the Order, however, shall prevent the Comptroller from:

(a) instituting enforcement actions, other than a civil money penalty, against the Bank based on the findings set forth in Article I of this Order;

(b) instituting enforcement actions against the Bank based on any other findings;

(c) instituting enforcement actions against the Bank's institution-affiliated parties based on the findings set forth in Article I of this Order, or any other findings; or

(d) utilizing the findings set forth in Article I of this Order in future enforcement actions against the Bank or its institution-affiliated parties to establish a pattern or the continuation of a pattern.

Further, nothing in the Stipulation or this Order shall affect any right of the Comptroller to determine and ensure compliance with the terms and provisions of the Stipulation or this Order.

(3) The terms of this Order, including this paragraph, are not subject to amendment or modification by any extraneous expression, prior agreements, or prior arrangements between the parties, whether oral or written.

IT IS SO ORDERED, this 29 th day of September , 2016.

  /s/ Greg J. Coleman
Greg J. Coleman
Deputy Comptroller
Large Bank Supervision

UNITED STATES OF AMERICA
DEPARTMENT OF THE TREASURY
COMPTROLLER OF THE CURRENCY

In the Matter of:	)))	AA-EC-2016-69
Wells Fargo Bank, N.A. Sioux Falls, South Dakota	))))	

STIPULATION AND CONSENT TO THE ISSUANCE
OF AN ORDER FOR A CIVIL MONEY PENALTY

WHEREAS, the Office of the Comptroller of the Currency ("OCC"), based upon information derived from the exercise of his regulatory and supervisory responsibilities, intends to initiate a civil money penalty proceeding against Wells Fargo Bank, N.A., Sioux Falls, South Dakota ("Bank") pursuant to 12 U.S.C. § 1818(i), for the Bank's violations of the Servicemembers Civil Relief Act ("SCRA"), 50 U.S.C. §§ 3901-4043;

WHEREAS, in the interest of cooperation and to avoid additional costs associated with administrative and judicial proceedings with respect to the above matter, the Bank, through its duly elected and acting Board of Directors ("Board"), has agreed to execute this Stipulation and Consent to the Issuance of a Civil Money Penalty ("Stipulation"), that is accepted by the OCC, through the duly authorized representative of the Comptroller of the Currency ("Comptroller");

NOW, THEREFORE, in consideration of the above premises, it is stipulated by the Bank that:

ARTICLE I

JURISDICTION

(1) The Bank is an "insured depository institution" as that term is defined in 12 U.S.C. § 1813(c)(2).

(2) The Bank is a "national banking association" within the meaning of 12 U.S.C. § 1813(q)(1)(A), and is chartered and examined by the OCC. *See* 12 U.S.C. § 1 *et seq.*

(3) The OCC is the "appropriate Federal banking agency" as that term is defined in 12 U.S.C. § 1813(q) and is therefore authorized to initiate and maintain this civil money penalty action against the Bank pursuant to 12 U.S.C. § 1818(i).

ARTICLE II

CONSENT

(1) The Bank, without admitting or denying any wrongdoing, consents and agrees to issuance of the accompanying Consent Order for a Civil Money Penalty ("Consent Order") by the OCC.

(2) The terms and provisions of the Consent Order apply to the Bank and all of its subsidiaries, even though those subsidiaries are not named as parties to the Consent Order.

(3) The Bank consents and agrees that the Consent Order shall be deemed an "order issued with the consent of the depository institution" pursuant to 12 U.S.C. § 1818(h)(2), and consents and agrees that the Consent Order shall become effective upon its execution by the OCC through the Comptroller's duly authorized representative, and shall be fully enforceable by the Comptroller pursuant to 12 U.S.C. § 1818(i).

(4) Notwithstanding the absence of mutuality of obligation, or of consideration, or of a contract, the OCC may enforce any of the commitments or obligations herein undertaken by the Bank under its supervisory powers, including 12 U.S.C. § 1818(i), and not as a matter of contract law. The Bank expressly acknowledges that neither the Bank nor the OCC has any intention to enter into a contract.

(5) The Bank declares that no separate promise or inducement of any kind has been made by the OCC, or by its officers, employees, or agents, to cause or induce the Bank to consent to the issuance of the Consent Order and/or execute this Stipulation.

(6) The Bank expressly acknowledges that no officer, employee, or agent of the OCC has statutory or other authority to bind the United States, the United States Treasury Department, the OCC, or any other federal bank regulatory agency or entity, or any officer, employee, or agent of any of those entities to a contract affecting the OCC's exercise of its supervisory responsibilities.

(7) The Consent Order constitutes a settlement of the civil money penalty proceeding against the Bank contemplated by the OCC, based on the violations of law described in the Comptroller's Findings set forth in Article I of the Consent Order. The OCC releases and discharges the Bank from all potential liability for a civil money penalty that has been or might have been asserted by the OCC based on the violations described in Article I of the Consent Order, to the extent known to the OCC as of the effective date of the Consent Order. Nothing in this Stipulation or the Consent Order, however, shall prevent the OCC from:

    (a) Instituting enforcement actions, other than a civil money penalty, against the Bank based on the findings set forth in Article I of the Consent Order;

(b) Instituting enforcement actions against the Bank based on any other findings;

(c) Instituting enforcement actions against the Bank's institution-affiliated parties based on the findings set forth in Article I of the Consent Order, or any other findings; or

(d) Utilizing the findings set forth in Article I of the Consent Order in future enforcement actions against the Bank or its institution-affiliated parties to establish a pattern or the continuation of a pattern.

Further, nothing in this Stipulation or the Consent Order shall affect any right of the OCC to determine and ensure compliance with the terms and provisions of this Stipulation or the Consent Order.

ARTICLE III

WAIVERS

(1) The Bank, by executing this Stipulation and consenting to the Consent Order, waives:

(a) Any and all rights to the issuance of a Notice of Charges pursuant to 12 U.S.C. § 1818(i);

(b) Any and all procedural rights available in connection with the issuance of the Consent Order;

(c) Any and all rights to a hearing and a final agency decision pursuant to 12 U.S.C. § 1818(i), and 12 C.F.R. Part 19;

(d) Any and all rights to seek any type of administrative or judicial review of the Consent Order;

(e) Any and all claims for fees, costs, or expenses against the OCC, or any officer, employee, or agent of the OCC, related in any way to this enforcement matter or the Consent Order, whether arising under common law or under the terms of any statute, including, but not limited to, the Equal Access to Justice Act, 5 U.S.C. § 504 and 28 U.S.C. § 2412; and

(f) Any and all rights to assert this proceeding, this Stipulation, consent to the issuance of the Consent Order, and/or the issuance of the Consent Order, as the basis for a claim of double jeopardy in any pending or future proceeding brought by the United States Department of Justice, or any other governmental entity; and

(g) Any and all rights to challenge or contest the validity of the Consent Order.

ARTICLE IV

CLOSING

(1) The provisions of this Stipulation and the Consent Order shall not inhibit, estop, bar, or otherwise prevent the OCC from taking any other action affecting the Bank if, at any time, the OCC deems it appropriate to do so to fulfill the responsibilities placed upon it by the several laws of the United States of America.

(2) Nothing in this Stipulation or the Consent Order shall preclude any proceedings brought by the OCC to enforce the terms of the Consent Order, and nothing in this Stipulation or

the Consent Order constitutes, nor shall the Bank contend that it constitutes, a release, discharge, compromise, settlement, dismissal, or resolution of any actions, or in any way affects any actions that may be or have been brought by any other representative of the United States or an agency thereof, including, without limitation, the United States Department of Justice.

(3)   The terms of this Stipulation, including this paragraph, and of the Consent Order are not subject to amendment or modification by any extraneous expression, prior agreements or prior arrangements between the parties, whether oral or written.

IN TESTIMONY WHEREOF, the undersigned, authorized by the Comptroller as his representative, has hereunto set his hand on behalf of the Comptroller.

/s/ Greg Coleman
Greg Coleman
Deputy Comptroller
Large Bank Supervision

9/29/16
Date

IN TESTIMONY WHEREOF, the undersigned, as the duly elected and acting Board of Directors of Wells Fargo Bank, N.A., Sioux Falls, South Dakota, have hereunto set their hands on behalf of the Bank.

/s/ John G. Stumpf September 29, 2016
John G. Stumpf   Date

/s/ Lloyd H. Dean September 29, 2016
Lloyd H. Dean   Date

/s/ Enrique Hernandez, Jr. September 29, 2016
Enrique Hernandez, Jr.   Date

/s/ Cynthia H. Milligan September 29, 2016
Cynthia H. Milligan   Date

/s/ Federico Peña September 29, 2016
Federico F. Peña   Date

/s/ James H. Quigley September 29, 2016
James H. Quigley   Date

/s/ Stephen Sanger September 29, 2016
Stephen W. Sanger   Date

LORETTA E. LYNCH
Attorney General
VANITA GUPTA
Principal Deputy Assistant Attorney General
SAMEENA SHINA MAJEED
Chief, Housing and Civil Enforcement Section
ELIZABETH A. SINGER
Director, U.S. Attorneys' Fair Housing Program
NICOLE M. SIEGEL
DANIEL P. MOSTELLER
Trial Attorneys
  U.S. Department of Justice
  Civil Rights Division
  Housing and Civil Enforcement Section
  950 Pennsylvania Ave. NW – NWB
  Washington, D.C. 20530
  Telephone: (202) 514-4713
  Facsimile: (202) 514-1116
  Email: daniel.mosteller@usdoj.gov

EILEEN M. DECKER
United States Attorney
DOROTHY A. SCHOUTEN
Assistant United States Attorney
Chief, Civil Division
JOANNA HULL (CA State Bar No. 227153)
Assistant United States Attorney
Chief, Civil Rights Section, Civil Division
  Federal Building, Suite 7516
  300 North Los Angeles Street
  Los Angeles, California 90012
  Telephone: (213) 894-6585
  Facsimile: (213) 894-7819
  E-mail: Joanna.Hull@usdoj.gov

Attorneys for Plaintiff
United States of America

UNITED STATES DISTRICT COURT

FOR THE CENTRAL DISTRICT OF CALIFORNIA

UNITED STATES OF AMERICA,
 	
  Plaintiff
 	
  v.
 	
WELLS FARGO BANK, N.A.
d/b/a
WELLS FARGO DEALER SERVICES
 	
  Defendant.
	No. CV 2:16-07336
	
	CONSENT ORDER

CONSENT ORDER

I. INTRODUCTION

1. This Consent Order resolves the allegations contained in the United States' Complaint that Defendant Wells Fargo Bank, N.A., d/b/a Wells Fargo Dealer Services ("Wells Fargo") violated the Servicemembers Civil Relief Act ("SCRA"), 50 U.S.C. § 3901, *et seq.*, when, according to the allegations, it engaged in a pattern or practice of repossessing motor vehicles from "SCRA-protected servicemembers"[1] without court orders from at least January 1, 2008 through July 1, 2015.

2. Defendant is a national bank whose motor vehicle lending operations are located at 23 Pasteur in Irvine, California, in the Central District of California.

3. This Order covers all loans or deficiency balances originated, acquired, and/or serviced by Defendant, its parent Wells Fargo & Company, or any of their subsidiaries, predecessors, acquired companies, or successor entities. For purposes of this Order, loans are defined to include retail installment contracts for motor vehicles.

4. Wells Fargo has cooperated fully with the United States' investigation in this matter and had taken steps to ensure its compliance with the SCRA, prior to this investigation. Wells Fargo established a centralized SCRA Center of Excellence that focuses specifically on SCRA compliance. The SCRA Center of Excellence employs a proactive approach to identifying servicemembers for SCRA protection. Wells Fargo initiated such efforts in the second quarter of 2014 with a full-scale review of its portfolio for SCRA

---

[1] For purposes of this Consent Order, the term "SCRA-protected servicemember" includes servicemembers as defined in 50 U.S.C. § 3911(1) and (2).

compliance. In addition, Wells Fargo previously and voluntarily commenced efforts to compensate any affected borrowers.

5. The parties agree that the Court has jurisdiction over the subject matter of this case pursuant to 28 U.S.C. § 1331, 28 U.S.C. § 1345, and 50 U.S.C. § 4041.

6. The parties agree that, to avoid costly and protracted litigation, the claims against Defendant should be resolved without further proceedings or an evidentiary hearing. Therefore, as indicated by the signatures appearing below, the United States and Defendant agree to the entry of this Order. Such agreement comes without the taking of proof and does not constitute evidence or findings against or an admission of any party regarding any issue of law or fact alleged in the Complaint. Defendant neither admits nor denies any of the allegations in the United States' Complaint.

7. The effective date of this Order will be the date on which it is approved and entered by the Court.

//

It is hereby ORDERED, ADJUDGED and DECREED:
II. REMEDIAL PROVISIONS[2]

8. Defendant and its affiliates or subsidiaries, and its officers, employees, agents, and representatives (including contractors and vendors that conduct repossessions on behalf of Defendant) shall comply fully with all relevant provisions of the SCRA prohibiting the repossession of motor vehicles of SCRA-protected servicemembers without a court order, while the servicemember is in military service[3], provided the servicemember paid a

---

[2] Nothing in this Consent Order shall preclude Defendant from offering greater protections to servicemembers than those afforded by the Consent Order or the SCRA.

[3] For purposes of this Consent Order, the term "military service" is defined by 50 U.S.C. § 3911(2).

deposit on the motor vehicle or installment on the loan while not in military service.[4]

III. COMPLIANCE WITH THE SCRA
AND SCRA POLICIES AND PROCEDURES

9. Within sixty (60) calendar days of the effective date of this Order, Defendant shall continue to develop SCRA Policies and Procedures for Motor Vehicle Repossessions in compliance with Section 3952(a) of the SCRA, 50 U.S.C. § 3952(a).[5] These policies and procedures must include provisions that ensure:

   a. In addition to any other reviews Defendant may perform to assess eligibility under the SCRA, (i) between two (2) and five (5) business days before it refers a motor vehicle loan for repossession; (ii) between two (2) and five (5) business days after it (or its agents, including contractors and vendors that conduct repossessions on behalf of Defendant) obtains possession of the motor vehicle; and (iii) between two (2) and five (5) business days before it (or its agents, including contractors and vendors that conduct repossessions on behalf of Defendant) disposes of the motor vehicle, Defendant will determine whether borrowers are servicemembers in military service who paid a deposit on the motor vehicle or installment on the loan while not in military service by: (1) reviewing any military service information (including orders) it has received from borrowers and (2)

---

[4] 50 U.S.C. § 3917 grants additional periods of protection for reservists ordered to report for military service and persons ordered to report for induction. Therefore, for purposes of this Consent Order, periods of protection granted by 50 U.S.C. § 3917 shall be considered "military service" at the time of repossession, but shall not be considered "military service" at the time of payment of a deposit on the motor vehicle or installment on the loan.

[5] Because Defendant's motor vehicle lending contracts do not obtain a security interest in the nature of a mortgage, which are subject to the requirements of Section 3953 of the SCRA, this Consent Order is limited to compliance with Section 3952(a) of the SCRA, which covers installment contracts.

searching the Department of Defense Manpower Data Center database ("DMDC") for evidence of SCRA eligibility by either (a) last name and social security number or (b) last name and date of birth.

b. If Defendant is informed via military service information received from a borrower, or via the periodic electronic check of the DMDC described above, that the borrower is a servicemember in military service who paid a deposit on the motor vehicle or installment on the loan while not in military service, it may refer the loan for repossession or conduct the repossession itself only after obtaining a court order.

c. If Defendant discovers, after obtaining possession but before disposing of the motor vehicle, that the borrower is a servicemember in military service who paid a deposit on the motor vehicle or installment on the loan while not in military service, Defendant shall attempt to contact the borrower and offer to arrange to return the vehicle as soon as possible, but within no later than seventy-two (72) hours, and shall reverse on the borrower's account all of the charges resulting from the repossession. Defendant shall also correct any negative credit reporting related to the repossession. If Defendant cannot make contact with the borrower within seventy-two (72) hours, Defendant shall cause the vehicle to be returned to the location where possession was taken, unless: (1) return to such location presents a significant risk of damage to the vehicle; (2) return to such location presents a significant risk that the vehicle will be impounded; (3) the borrower has previously informed Defendant that the vehicle has been abandoned; or (4) the vehicle was recovered under circumstances suggesting that the vehicle had been abandoned. If the vehicle is not returned to the borrower within seventy-two (72) hours, Defendant shall make 3 additional attempts to reach the borrower based upon contact information in its files, and return the vehicle as soon as possible, but within no later than seventy-two (72) hours, of a borrower's request for return, without charging storage fees. The vehicle may only be sold or otherwise disposed of only after the contact attempts referenced in this subparagraph have been made.

    d.   If Defendant pursues a repossession action in court and the borrower fails to answer the action, Defendant will file an affidavit of military service with the court as required by Section 3931(b)(1) of the SCRA, 50 U.S.C. § 3931(b)(1). Before seeking entry of default, Defendant will search the DMDC and review information in its possession or control to determine if the borrower is SCRA-protected. If Defendant learns that the borrower is SCRA-protected, Defendant will: (1) file an affidavit stating that "the defendant is in military service" before seeking default judgment; and (2) attach the most recent military status report from the DMDC or a copy of the military orders or other documentation to the affidavit.

    e.   Defendant may only rely on a servicemember's waiver of rights under Section 3952(a) of the SCRA if it obtains a written agreement as provided in Section 3918 of the SCRA, 50 U.S.C. § 3918. If Defendant makes an unsolicited initiation of the waiver process with the servicemember, it must do so at least thirty (30) calendar days in advance of any anticipated repossession by sending a notice and a copy of the proposed waiver to the servicemember. To the extent

Defendant exercises this right, Defendant shall use a notice that prominently incorporates the language and layout of the form attached as Exhibit A. If the servicemember initiates the waiver process by offering to voluntarily surrender the vehicle or indicating an intent to abandon the vehicle, Defendant must provide a copy of the notice of the type described in Exhibit A and may obtain possession of the vehicle at any point after receiving a signed waiver.

f. Defendant may take possession of a motor vehicle that has been impounded by a non-related third-party or abandoned[6] upon receiving notice of the impoundment or abandonment even when the borrower is a servicemember in military service who paid a deposit on the motor vehicle or installment on the loan while not in military service. Defendant must, however, provide notice to the servicemember that it has taken possession and inform the servicemember of the rights and protections under the SCRA, using a notice that prominently incorporates the language and layout of the form attached as Exhibit A. Defendant may dispose of the vehicle only after such notice and any notice required by state law have been provided and at least thirty (30) calendar days have passed.

10. Within sixty (60) calendar days of the effective date of this Order, Defendant shall continue to develop SCRA Policies and Procedures for Providing SCRA Relief in its motor vehicle lending line of business. This includes, but is not

---

[6] To be considered "abandoned" under this Order, the motor vehicle must have been left someplace other than the servicemember's residence or residential parking area, with indications of no intent to retrieve it.

limited to, policies regarding reducing interest rates under Section 3937.[7]
The Policies and Procedures shall contain the following provisions:

    a.   Defendant shall accept servicemembers' notice of military status pursuant to the SCRA (including provisions of the SCRA that require notice in order to receive relief) made via facsimile, United States Postal Service First Class Mail (postage pre-paid), overnight mail, or electronically.

    b.   Defendant shall designate customer service representatives who have been specifically trained on the protections of the SCRA and who are responsible for the intake of and response to servicemembers' inquiries regarding the SCRA. Defendant shall ensure that it has a designated telephone number, and electronic mail address, at which servicemembers may reach the designated SCRA customer service representatives, who will address questions or concerns regarding relief pursuant to the SCRA. Defendant shall also include a page on its website detailing eligibility for, and relief provided by, the SCRA, and providing the designated telephone number and electronic mail address to obtain SCRA relief, or raise questions or concerns regarding such relief.

    c.   When Defendant receives notice from a servicemember of military status pursuant to the SCRA, within sixty (60) calendar days, it shall review all the servicemember's loans, regardless of type of obligation, even if it is outside the motor vehicle lending line of business, and it shall determine the servicemember's eligibility for all forms of relief pursuant to the SCRA on all loans. If the

---

[7] The SCRA Policies and Procedures for Providing SCRA Relief need not include early termination of leases under Section 3955 so long as Defendant is not the business of leasing motor vehicles.

servicemember is determined to be eligible, the relief will be applied retroactively to the first day of eligibility.

d. Within twenty (20) business days after determining a servicemember's eligibility for relief pursuant to the SCRA, Defendant shall notify the servicemember in writing[8] of its determination. If Defendant grants relief, Defendant shall notify the servicemember in writing of the specific terms of the relief provided. If Defendant denies relief, Defendant shall also notify the servicemember in writing of the reason(s) for the denial, and it shall ensure that such servicemember is given an opportunity to provide additional documentation or information to establish eligibility for relief pursuant to the SCRA.

e. With respect to forms of relief for which the SCRA requires provision of military orders, in the event that a servicemember fails to provide a copy of military orders entitling him or her to the relief, Defendant shall search the DMDC to confirm eligibility. If the DMDC records provide dates of service that confirm eligibility, Defendant shall provide the relief required by the SCRA for the dates indicated by the DMDC and shall notify the servicemember that the servicemember may submit additional documentation to establish eligibility dates if the servicemember disagrees with the dates provided by the DMDC. If the DMDC records do not confirm

---

[8] For all written notices to servicemembers required by the Consent Order, Defendant shall use either: (1) the email address or mailing address chosen by the borrower as the primary means of communication either by previous election or in the most recent communication with the Defendant; or (2) if, no primary means of communication has been chosen, the mailing and e-mail address listed in the servicemember's most recent communication with Defendant, in addition to the servicemember's current mailing address in Defendant's servicing records (if different).

eligibility, Defendant may deny the relief if it informs the servicemember in writing that he or she is not eligible for the relief unless he or she provides a copy of documents establishing military service. Such documents will include any document prepared exclusively by a branch of the military, the Department of Defense, or a borrower's commanding officer that indicates that the borrower is on active duty (e.g., active duty orders, change of station orders, DD-214 forms, letters from commanding officers, etc.). Defendant shall request this additional information before making a final determination that the servicemember is not eligible for relief.

f. Defendant shall accept military orders without requiring a specific end date for the period of military service. Defendant also shall accept military orders without requiring the specification of the date upon which the servicemember first entered active duty for this period of service.

g. Defendant shall provide SCRA relief beginning on the earliest eligible date provided in the orders or by the DMDC. However, if the earliest date provided indicates that the servicemember was on active duty at the time of loan origination, Defendant shall notify the servicemember that he or she has been declined for the protection, but shall provide the servicemember a reasonable opportunity to provide documentation showing that the servicemember was not on active duty at the time of loan origination.

h. Defendant shall be permitted to discontinue relief granted pursuant to the SCRA only after Defendant searches the DMDC and the DMDC reports that the servicemember is not in military service (or in any

SCRA-protected period after the termination of military service).[9] Defendant shall notify the servicemember in writing of the discontinuation, and it shall ensure that such servicemember is given an opportunity to provide additional documentation or information to reestablish eligibility for relief pursuant to the SCRA. Defendant may choose to provide relief for a longer period than is required by this subparagraph.

    i. The Policies and Procedures required by this Paragraph do not excuse Defendant from providing, or allow Defendant to delay providing, forms of relief for which the SCRA does not require a notification from a servicemember. For example, the Policies and Procedures required by this Paragraph do not affect the timing requirement of Paragraph 9.

11. No later than sixty (60) calendar days after the effective date of this Order, Defendant shall provide a copy of the proposed SCRA Policies and Procedures required under Paragraphs 9 and 10 to counsel for the United States.[10] The United States shall respond to Defendant's proposed SCRA Policies and Procedures within forty-five (45) calendar days of receipt. If the United States objects to any part of Defendant's SCRA Policies and Procedures, the parties shall confer to resolve their differences. If the parties cannot resolve their differences after good faith efforts to do so, either party

---

[9] In the case where an SCRA-protected servicemember provides Defendant with valid military orders that include an end date of military service inconsistent with that appearing in the DMDC, Defendant may only discontinue the relief after the latter of the two end dates has expired or it obtains confirmation from the borrower that he or she has ended military service.

[10] All materials required by this Consent Order to be sent to counsel for the United States shall be sent by commercial overnight delivery addressed as follows: Chief, Housing and Civil Enforcement Section, Civil Rights Division, U.S. Department of Justice, 1800 G Street, N.W., 7th Floor, Washington, DC 20006, Attn: DJ 216-12C-2.

may bring the dispute to this Court for resolution. Defendant shall begin the process of implementing the SCRA Policies and Procedures within ten (10) calendar days of approval by the United States or the Court.

12. If, at any time during the term of this Order, Defendant proposes to materially change its SCRA Policies and Procedures described herein, it shall first provide a copy of the proposed changes to counsel for the United States. If the United States does not deliver written objections to Defendant within forty-five (45) calendar days of receiving the proposed changes, the changes may be implemented. If the United States makes any objections to the proposed changes within the forty-five (45)-day period, the specific changes to which the United States objects shall not be implemented until the objections are resolved pursuant to the process described in Paragraph 11.

IV. TRAINING

13. Defendant shall provide additional SCRA compliance training to any employees who: (a) provide customer service to servicemembers in connection with the servicing of motor vehicle loans, (b) have significant involvement in servicing motor vehicle loans, including the ability to reduce interest rates or terminate motor vehicle leases for servicemembers as contemplated by the terms of the SCRA, or (c) have significant involvement in repossessions of motor vehicles, (hereinafter together "covered employees") within forty-five (45) calendar days after Defendant's training program is approved by the United States or the Court pursuant to Paragraph 15. Defendant shall provide to each covered employee: (a) training on the terms of the SCRA specific to the employee's responsibilities associated with that employee's position; (b) training on the terms of Defendant's SCRA Policies and Procedures (both those required pursuant to Paragraph 9 and 10, and all others adopted by Defendant) specific to the employee's

responsibilities associated with that employee's position; (c) training on the terms of this Order specific to the employee's responsibilities associated with that employee's position and his or her responsibilities and obligations under the SCRA; and (d) the contact information for the SCRA customer service representatives described in Paragraph 10(b). Defendant shall also follow these training procedures for all of their employees who subsequently become covered employees within thirty (30) calendar days of their hiring, promotion or transfer.

14. During the term of this Order, Defendant shall continue to provide annual SCRA training, with the same content as described in Paragraph 13, to covered employees with respect to their responsibilities and obligations under the SCRA, the SCRA Policies and Procedures and the terms of this Order.

15. Within forty-five (45) calendar days of the United States' approval of the SCRA Policies and Procedures pursuant to Paragraphs 9 and 10, Defendant shall provide to the United States the curriculum, instructions, and any written material included in the training required by Paragraphs 13 and 14. These materials may incorporate SCRA compliance training offered on or before the effective date of this Order. The United States shall have forty-five (45) calendar days from receipt of these documents to raise any objections to Defendant's training materials, and, if it raises any, the parties shall confer to resolve their differences. In the event they are unable to do so, either party may bring the dispute to this Court for resolution.

16. The covered employees may undergo the training required by Paragraphs 13 and 14 via live training, computer-based training, web-based training, or via interactive digital media. If the training is conducted in any format other than live training, Defendant shall ensure that covered employees have the opportunity to have their questions answered by a company contact that

Defendant identifies as having SCRA expertise within two (2) business days of the training. The training must require the covered employees to verify their participation. If the training is conducted in any format other than live training, the training must require that covered employees demonstrate proficiency. Any expenses associated with the training program required by Paragraphs 13 and 14 shall be borne by Defendant.

17. Defendant shall certify in writing to counsel for the United States that covered employees successfully completed the training required by Paragraphs 13 and 14 and that said employees received the Consent Order and the SCRA Policies and Procedures specific to the employee's responsibilities associated with the loan being serviced. Additionally, Defendant shall maintain a list of all covered employees who successfully completed the training required by Paragraphs 13 and 14. For the duration of this Order, copies of this list shall be provided to the United States upon request.

V. COMPENSATION

18. Defendant will deposit in an interest-bearing escrow account the sum of $4,130,000 to fund the compensation payments required by Paragraph 22. Title to this account will be in the name of "Wells Fargo Bank, N.A. d/b/a Wells Fargo Dealer Services for the benefit of affected persons pursuant to Order of the Court in Civil Action No. [XXX]". Defendant will provide written verification of the deposit to the United States within fifteen (15) calendar days of the effective date of this Order. Any interest that accrues will become part of the Settlement Fund and be used and disposed of as set forth herein. If the compensation payments required by Paragraph 22 total more than $4,130,000, Defendant will deposit into the escrow account all necessary additional funds to make payments before the deadlines established

by Paragraph 27. Any taxes, costs, or other fees related to the escrow account shall be paid by Defendant.

19. In the event Defendant determines that there are additional repossession accounts that were not in compliance with the SCRA, Defendant will undertake remedial compensation actions on those accounts while this Order is in effect and in a similar manner as outlined in this Order.

20. The United States has determined that Defendant conducted 413 motor vehicle repossessions between January 1, 2008 and July 1, 2015 that were not in compliance with the SCRA; Defendant maintains that 31 of these were not violations of the SCRA, however Defendant has agreed to remediate these 31 repossessions in the interest of compromise. The United States has previously provided the list of these repossessions to Defendant.

21. Within thirty (30) calendar days of the effective date of this Order, Defendant shall provide to the United States an electronically searchable list of all its repossessions between July 2, 2015 and the effective date of this Order. The United States shall run this list through the DMDC and undertake any independent investigation it deems appropriate to identify any additional repossessions that were not in compliance with the SCRA. The United States shall provide Defendant with the list of additional repossessions that were not in compliance with SCRA within thirty (30) calendar days of receiving Defendant's complete repossession list. In the event Defendant objects to the United States' list, Defendant shall be afforded thirty (30) calendar days to produce evidence of compliance to the United States. After considering in good faith all evidence produced by Defendant, the United States shall make a final determination of the additional repossessions that were not in compliance with the SCRA within thirty (30) calendar day of Defendant's production of evidence.

22. For each non-SCRA compliant repossession identified pursuant to Paragraphs 20 and 21, Defendant shall provide the following compensation:

    a. an amount of $10,000;

    b. any lost equity in the repossessed motor vehicle, as calculated by: subtracting any outstanding principal, interest, and other amounts owing by the borrowers (excluding any fees associated with repossession), plus any liens at the time of repossession and any disbursements made to the servicemember or a third party other than a lien holder from the proceeds of the repossession sale (exclusive of any fees associated with the repossession) from the retail value of the motor vehicle at the time of repossession as identified in the National Automobile Dealers Association ("NADA") Guide; and

    c. interest accrued on this lost equity, calculated from the date of the repossession sale until the date payment is issued, at the rate set forth in 28 U.S.C. § 1961.

Defendant shall provide the United States with all records used to make the payment calculations described in this Paragraph for the United States' review and approval.

23. The amounts described in Paragraph 22(a) shall be paid entirely to the servicemember-borrower on the note securing the motor vehicle. Defendant may require the servicemember-borrower to sign the Declaration at Exhibit B-1 and/or the Release at Exhibit B-2. Defendant may require any non-servicemember co-borrowers to sign the Release at Exhibit B-2. The amounts described in Paragraph 22(b) and (c) shall be distributed equally among all borrowers (including non-servicemember borrowers) on the title to the motor vehicle who sign the Declaration at Exhibit B-1, if required, and the Release at Exhibit B-2. In cases where Defendant has already taken

remedial actions with respect to a repossession identified pursuant to Paragraphs 20 and 21, the United States shall consider such remedial actions and adjust the compensation to be awarded.[11]

24. Within sixty (60) calendar days of the effective date of this Order, Defendant shall submit a plan ("Remediation Plan") to provide for the administration of borrower compensation. Pursuant to the Remediation Plan, Defendant shall conduct the activities set forth in Paragraphs 24-28. The terms of the Remediation Plan shall be subject to the non-objection of the United States. Defendant shall bear all costs and expenses of implementing the Remediation Plan. The Remediation Plan shall require Defendant to work cooperatively with the United States in the conduct of its activities, including reporting regularly to and providing all reasonably requested information to the United States.

25. Defendant, as part of its Remediation Plan, shall establish, and maintain throughout the contract period, cost-free means for affected servicemembers to contact it, including an electronic mail address, a website, and a toll-free telephone number.

26. For non-SCRA compliant repossessions identified pursuant to Paragraph 20, Defendant shall, to the extent it has not already, notify each identified servicemember by letter (using wording mutually agreeable to Defendant and the United States) within sixty (60) calendar days of the effective date of this Order. After the United States' determination, as provided in Paragraph 21,

---

[11] In determining the amount of compensation due to any servicemember or co-borrower pursuant to Paragraph 22, the United States will credit any monetary compensation or other remediation efforts, including returning the motor vehicle to the borrower, already provided to any servicemember or co-borrower for alleged compliance issues pursuant to Section 3952 of the SCRA and arising from the same motor vehicle loan.

Defendant shall notify each identified servicemember by letter (using wording mutually agreeable to Defendant and the United States) within forty-five (45) calendar days of the United States' determination. For repossessions where money is due to a non-servicemember borrower pursuant to Paragraph 22, Defendant shall notify each identified non-servicemember borrower by letter (using wording mutually agreeable to Defendant and the United States) within fifteen (15) calendar days of receiving the Declaration, if required, and Release from the servicemember-borrower. Defendant shall provide the United States with samples of all letters, and receive the United States' approval of the sample letters, before mailing any letter required by this Paragraph, and all letters mailed pursuant to this Paragraph shall be accompanied by the Declaration at Exhibit B-1, if required, and the Release at Exhibit B-2. The Remediation Plan shall set forth effective methods to make contact with, and obtain a response from, each identified servicemember and non-servicemember borrower.

27. Defendant shall issue and mail compensation checks no later than twenty-one (21) calendar days after receipt of a signed declaration, if required, and release. Defendant shall skip trace and redeliver any payment that is returned to Defendant as undeliverable, or that is not deposited or cashed within six (6) months.

28. Defendant shall for a period of two (2) years following the effective date of this Order provide the United States with a monthly accounting of all declarations, if required, and releases received, checks issued (including copies of issued checks), and notifications without responses or that were returned as undeliverable. Defendant shall report any uncashed checks in accordance with state unclaimed property laws.

29. Any money not distributed from the escrow account, including accrued interest, within two (2) years of the date the initial notifications are sent to persons eligible for the compensation payments required by Paragraph 22 will be distributed to one or more charitable organizations that assist servicemembers. Recipient(s) of such funds must not be related to Defendant. Before selecting the organization(s), Defendant will obtain a proposal from the organization(s) on how the funds will be used consistent with furthering the goals of the SCRA, submit such proposal to the United States, and consult with and obtain the non-objection of the United States. The United States and Defendant may request modification of the proposal before approving the organization(s). The parties will thereafter seek approval from the Court to distribute the remaining funds to the qualified organization(s). Defendant will require each recipient to submit to Defendant and the United States a detailed report on how funds are utilized within one (1) year after the funds are distributed, and every year thereafter until the funds are exhausted.

30. Defendant will be entitled to a set-off, or any other reduction, of the amount of compensation payments required by Paragraph 22 because of any debts owed by the recipient, only in the calculation of lost equity as provided by Paragraph 22(b). Defendant also will make payments notwithstanding any release of legal claims, arbitration agreement, or loan modification previously signed by any such recipient.

31. In the event that the United States has reason to believe that Defendant is not materially complying with the terms of the Remediation Plan, Defendant shall present for review and determination of non-objection a course of action to effectuate material compliance with the Remediation Plan. The United States shall make a determination of non-objection to the course of action or

direct Defendant to revise it. In the event that the United States directs revisions, Defendant shall make the revisions and resubmit the course of action to the United States within thirty (30) days. Upon notification that the United States has made a determination of non-objection, Defendant shall implement the course of action. If the parties cannot resolve differences with regard to the revised course of action after good faith efforts to do so, either party may bring the dispute to this Court for resolution. No individual may obtain review by the Court or the parties of the identifications made, and payments disbursed, pursuant to Paragraphs 20-28.

VI. OTHER RELIEF

32. Concurrent with providing financial compensation to the servicemember-borrower, Defendant must request that all three (3) major credit bureaus delete trade lines for accounts belonging to the servicemember(s) and any co-borrower(s) attributable specifically to the wrongful repossessions. Further, Defendant shall abandon, and must indemnify the servicemember and his or her co-borrower(s) against any third-party's pursuing, any claim for deficiency that was remaining on the SCRA-protected loan after a repossession, where the repossession was allegedly completed in violation of the SCRA by Defendant.

33. Every quarter for a period of two (2) years following the effective date of this Order, Defendant shall provide the United States with an accounting of all credit entries repaired.

VII. CIVIL PENALTY

34. Within thirty (30) calendar days of the effective date of this Order, Defendant shall pay a total of Sixty Thousand Dollars ($60,000) to the United States Treasury as a civil penalty pursuant to 50 U.S.C. § 4041(b)(3) and 28 C.F.R. 85.3(b)(4), to vindicate the public interest. The payment shall be in the form

of an electronic funds transfer pursuant to written instructions to be provided by the United States.

VIII. ADDITIONAL REPORTING AND RECORD-KEEPING REQUIREMENTS

35. For the duration of this Order, Defendant shall retain all records relating to its obligations hereunder, including its records with respect to all loans for which a servicemember has sought SCRA relief, whether that relief was granted by Defendant, all records involving repossessions, and all records relating to compliance activities as set forth herein. The United States shall have the right to review and copy any such records, including electronic data, upon reasonable request during the term of this Order.

36. During the term of this Order, Defendant shall notify counsel for the United States in writing every six (6) months of receipt of any SCRA or military-related complaint by the motor vehicle lending line of business. Defendant shall provide a copy of any written complaints with the notifications. Defendant will incorporate into its SCRA Policies and Procedures a requirement that all customer service personnel, upon receiving any oral SCRA complaint, shall notify individuals designated and trained to receive SCRA complaints pursuant to Paragraph 10(b). Whether regarding a written or oral SCRA complaint, the notification to the United States shall include the full details of the complaint, including the complainant's name, address, and telephone number, and the full details of all actions Defendant took to resolve the complaint. Defendant shall also promptly provide the United States all information it may request concerning any such complaint. If the United States raises any objections to Defendant's actions, the parties shall meet and confer to consider appropriate steps to address the concerns raised by the United States' review. If the parties are unable to come to an

agreement regarding such objections or concerns, either party may bring the dispute to this Court for resolution.

IX. SCOPE OF CONSENT ORDER

37. The provisions of this Order shall apply to Defendant, its parent Wells Fargo & Company, and any of their subsidiaries, predecessors, acquired companies, or successor entities. It shall also apply to the officers, employees, agents, representatives, assigns, successors-in-interest, and all persons and entities in active concert or participation with all of those entities, including with respect to any loans they acquired from January 1, 2008 to the effective date of this Order.

38. In the event that Defendant is acquired by or merges with another entity, Defendant shall, as a condition of such acquisition or merger, obtain the written agreement of the acquiring or surviving entity to be bound by any obligations remaining under this Order for the remaining term of this Order.

39. This Order does not release claims for practices not addressed in the Complaint's allegations, and it does not resolve and release claims other than those under Section 3952(a) of the SCRA. This Order does not release any claims that may be held or are currently under investigation by any federal agency, or any claims that may be pursued for actions that may be taken by any executive agency established by 12 U.S.C. § 5491 or the appropriate Federal Banking Agency (FBA), as defined in 12 U.S.C. § 1813(q), against Defendant, Wells Fargo & Company, any of their affiliated entities, and/or any their institution-affiliated parties, as defined by 12 U.S.C. § 1818 or any other statute or regulation.

40. Nothing in this Order will excuse Defendant's compliance with any currently or subsequently effective provision of law or order of a regulator with authority over Defendant that imposes additional obligations on it.

41. The parties agree that, as of the effective date of this Order, litigation is not "reasonably foreseeable" concerning the matters described above. To the extent that either party previously implemented a litigation hold to preserve documents, electronically stored information (ESI), or things related to the matters described above, the party is no longer required to maintain such litigation hold. Nothing in this Paragraph relieves either party of any other obligations imposed by this Order.

X. MODIFICATIONS, ATTORNEY'S FEES AND COSTS, AND REMEDIES FOR NON-COMPLIANCE

42. Any time limits for performance imposed by this Order may be extended by the mutual written agreement of the parties.

43. The parties shall be responsible for their own attorney's fees and court costs, except as provided for in Paragraph 45.

44. The parties shall endeavor in good faith to resolve informally any differences regarding the interpretation of and compliance with this Order prior to bringing such matters to the Court for resolution. However, in the event the United States contends that there has been a failure by Defendant, whether willful or otherwise, to perform in a timely manner any act required by this Order or otherwise comply with any provision thereof, the United States may move the Court to impose any remedy authorized by law or equity, including, but not limited to, an order requiring the performance of such act or deeming such act to have been performed, and an award of any damages, costs, and attorney's fees which may have been occasioned by Defendant's violation or failure to perform.

XI. RETENTION OF JURISDICTION

45. As described in Paragraph 4, for the past two and one-half years, Defendant has been engaged in large-scale voluntary SCRA compliance efforts. This

Order shall be in effect for an additional period of two and one-half years from its date of entry. The Court shall retain jurisdiction for the duration of this Order to enforce its terms, after which time this case shall be dismissed with prejudice. The United States may move the Court to extend the duration of this Order in the interests of justice.

SO ORDERED, this ___ day of _____, 2016.

_____
UNITED STATES DISTRICT JUDGE

The undersigned hereby apply for and consent to the entry of the Order:

For the United States of America:

EILEEN M. DECKER United States Attorney	LORETTA E. LYNCH Attorney General
DOROTHY A. SCHOUTEN Assistant United States Attorney Chief, Civil Division	VANITA GUPTA Principal Deputy Assistant Attorney General Civil Rights Division
/s/ *Joanna Hull* JOANNA HULL Assistant United States Attorney Chief, Civil Rights Section	/s/ *Sameena Shina Majeed* SAMEENA SHINA MAJEED Chief, Housing and Civil Enforcement Section
	/s/ *Elizabeth A. Singer* ELIZABETH A. SINGER Director, U.S. Attorneys' Fair Housing Program
	/s/ *Daniel P. Mosteller* NICOLE M. SIEGEL DANIEL P. MOSTELLER Trial Attorneys

For Defendant Wells Fargo Bank, N.A., d/b/a Wells Fargo Dealer Services:

/s/ Erin J. Illman
ERIN J. ILLMAN (CA No. 238262)
BRADLEY ARANT BOULT CUMMINGS LLP
214 N. Tyron Street, Suite 3700
Charlotte, NC 28202
Phone: (704) 338-6123
Fax: (704) 332-8858
eillman@bradley.com

ROBERT R. MADDOX
KEITH S. ANDERSON
ALISON C. SMITH
BRADLEY ARANT BOULT CUMMINGS LLP
One Federal Place
1819 Fifth Avenue North
Birmingham, AL 35203
Phone: (205) 521-8000
Fax: (205) 521-8800
rmaddox@bradley.com
kanderson@bradley.com
acsmith@bradley.com

The undersigned hereby apply for and consent to the entry of the Order:

For the United States of America:

EILEEN M. DECKER
United States Attorney

DOROTHY A. SCHOUTEN
Assistant United States Attorney
Chief, Civil Division

/s/ *Joanna Hull*
JOANNA HULL
Assistant United States Attorney
Chief, Civil Rights Section

LORETTA E. LYNCH
Attorney General

VANITA GUPTA
Principal Deputy
Assistant Attorney General
Civil Rights Division

SAMEENA SHINA MAJEED
Chief, Housing and Civil Enforcement Section

ELIZABETH A. SINGER
Director, U.S. Attorneys' Fair Housing Program

NICOLE M. SIEGEL
DANIEL P. MOSTELLER
Trial Attorneys

For Defendant Wells Fargo Bank, N.A., d/b/a Wells Fargo Dealer Services:

signature

ERIN J. ILLMAN (CA No. 238262)
BRADLEY ARANT BOULT CUMMINGS LLP
214 N. Tyron Street, Suite 3700
Charlotte, NC 28202
Phone: (704) 338-6123
Fax: (704) 332-8858
eillman@bradley.com

ROBERT R. MADDOX
KEITH S. ANDERSON
ALISON C. SMITH
BRADLEY ARANT BOULT CUMMINGS LLP
One Federal Place
1819 Fifth Avenue North
Birmingham, AL 35203
Phone: (205) 521-8000
Fax: (205) 521-8800
rmaddox@bradley.com
kanderson@bradley.com
acsmith@bradley.com

EXHIBIT A

IMPORTANT NOTICE AFFECTING MILITARY SERVICEMEMBERS

RIGHTS AND PROTECTIONS AFFORDED UNDER THE SERVICEMEMBERS

CIVIL RELIEF ACT

Attached to this notice you will find a waiver of rights and protections that may be applicable to you and your dependents pursuant to the Servicemembers Civil Relief Act, 50 U.S.C. § 3901, et seq. (the "SCRA"). The SCRA provides military personnel and their dependents with a wide range of legal and financial protections. Among other benefits and protections, the SCRA:

- Prohibits the repossession of a servicemember's motor vehicle without a court order, as long as a deposit or at least one installment payment was made while the borrower was not in military service.
- Upon notice by the servicemember, imposes a 6% maximum rate of interest that may be charged during military service on loans incurred before the servicemember began his or her current military service.
- Postpones court actions against servicemembers under certain circumstances.

If you choose to sign the attached waiver, Wells Fargo will have the option to proceed with a repossession of your motor vehicle without the protections of the SCRA. If you do not sign this waiver, Wells Fargo will be required to obtain a court order to repossess if you took out your loan and made a down payment on the motor vehicle, or at least one payment on the loan, when you were not in military service. You may be able to seek a postponement of the repossession. Additionally, if Wells Fargo takes you to court to repossess your motor vehicle, the court may take steps to ensure that a judgment is not entered against you if you are unable to appear.

Before waiving these important statutory rights, you should consult an attorney regarding how best to exercise your rights or whether it is in your interest to waive these rights under the conditions offered by Wells Fargo.

For More Information:

- CONSULT AN ATTORNEY: To fully understand your rights under the law, and before waiving your rights, you should consult an attorney.
- JAG / LEGAL ASSISTANCE: Servicemembers and their dependents with questions about the SCRA should contact their unit's Judge Advocate, or their installation's Legal Assistance Officer. A military legal assistance office locator for all branches of the Armed Forces is available at http://legalassistance.law.af.mil/content/locator.php.
- MILITARY ONESOURCE: "Military OneSource" is the U.S. Department of Defense's information resource. Go to http://www.militaryonesource.com.

EXHIBIT B-1
DECLARATION

I, [INSERT NAME], do hereby declare and state as follows:

1. I owned a vehicle obtained through a loan with Wells Fargo, Loan Number [LOAN NUMBER] that was repossessed.
2. I obtained the loan on or about [LOAN FUNDING DATE].
3. On or about [REPOSSESSION DATE], I WAS either:
   i. on a covered period of military service; OR
   ii. a member of a reserve component (Reserves or National Guard) and had received orders to report for a covered period of military service.
4. Please consider the following additional information in support of this Declaration:

_____

_____

_____

_____

_____

I confirm that the foregoing is true and correct.

Executed this _____ day of _____, 20__.

SIGNATURE: _____

PRINT NAME: _____

APPENDIX REGARDING MILITARY SERVICE

As used in this Declaration, a "covered period of military service" is any of the following:

    a) Full-time active duty with the armed forces of the United States (Army, Navy, Air Force, Marine Corps, or Coast Guard);

    b) A period of active service with the National Guard: i) authorized by the President or the Secretary of Defense; ii) longer than thirty (30) consecutive days; iii) under orders issued under Section 502(f) of Title 32 of the United States Code; and iv) for the purpose of responding to a national emergency declared by the President and supported by federal funds;

    c) Active service as a commissioned officer of the Public Health Service or the National Oceanic and Atmospheric Administration; or

    d) A period of time during which I was a servicemember absent from duty on account of sickness, wounds, leave, or other lawful cause.

If you have any additional questions about whether your service constitutes a "covered period of military service" for purposes of this declaration, please contact the Department of Justice at 202-514-4713 and reference the Wells Fargo SCRA motor vehicle case.

EXHIBIT B-2

SETTLEMENT AND GENERAL RELEASE AGREEMENT

In consideration for Wells Fargo Bank, N.A., d/b/a Wells Fargo Dealer Services' payment to me of $[AMOUNT], I, [BORROWER'S NAME], hereby release and forever discharge all claims, arising prior to the date of this Agreement, related to alleged violations of Section 3952(a) of the Servicemembers Civil Relief Act in the repossession and sale of a [VEHICLE; VIN_____] that I may have against Wells Fargo and all related entities, parents, predecessors, successors, subsidiaries, and affiliates and all of its past and present directors, officers, agents, managers, supervisors, shareholders, and employees and its heirs, executors, administrators, successors or assigns.

The parties represent and warrant to each other, that the parties specifically understand and agree that the parties' settlement and compromise claims and disputes regarding the retail installment contract and the vehicle is a compromise of disputed claims and that the existence of this Agreement or any payment made hereunder shall not be construed as an admission of liability of the allegations, claims or contentions of any party, and that there are no covenants, promises, undertakings or understanding between the parties outside of this Agreement except as specifically set forth herein.

Executed this _____ day of _____, 20___.

SIGNATURE: _____

PRINT NAME: _____

www.ingramcontent.com/pod-product-compliance
Lightning Source LLC
Chambersburg PA
CBHW080609190526
45169CB00007B/2943